published 2016 by Northern Undercurrents

ISBN 978-0-9958247-0-6

cover artwork by Bianca Martin

In celebration of Andrew,

and to honour all those

with quiet wisdom,

including Earl.

I walked quickly
forging ahead
while puppy
ambled and thrust

I was trying to make up
lost time
move muscles
too long rusty

and time
did her sinewy dance
retracting and stretching
and never lost

at some point
before my feet
massaged gaia

aspens had surrendered
to shaking by wind
festooning their green friends
before another sleep

everywhere I looked,
needles adorned with gold,
a party I almost missed.

Two eagles
twisting in air
talons gripped

feet hooked
in a mating flight
plunging to earth

risking death
in a crazy commitment to life

what urge of evolution
provoked this mad entwining?

Shenpa embodied
a powerful tangle

they swoop with desolate love
towards hard ground

we can hardly bear
to watch,
fear of waste so strong

ripped feathers
and screaming…

life itself,
some will to co-create,
a serendipitous breeze
soothes them
before impact,
turns descent
to separate sets of wings
pulling for flight

these regal eyes
seeing far from new heights

and I swear to god
they're laughing.

with thanks to The Bennett Sun

Those beautiful women
singing

each with her frailty
lighting her face

yearning and delight
in nimble fingers
strumming and plucking

a sweet kindness
of pine trees
more real than hothouse rose;

weaving an invitation,

gently commanding our yes.

That beautiful eagle
swirling
with his wings spread wide

white and black plumage
exposed proudly
for all of us

all that power
dancing

that strength
pounding rhythm into ground
to move us

that patient beauty
carving itself free.

We will see him
overhead
even through our blurry tears

feel earth shake
with his laughter

share the pain of his departure

the joy of his being.

I want to be
a luminous geezer

honouring the wise ones
striding through their end days

knowing they do not end

hiding their striding
in gentle steps

with strong voices
quavering brave

speaking truths
distilled
by global agony
and years of practice

sweating
sweet drops of possibility

fierce exhortations
to keep moving.

Let me watch the earth
play bocce by herself

let me set down
these beautiful balls

I have juggled too long

see them nestled
in the ground
that holds them

watch them roll
or sit

with the tilting belly
of gaia

release my fear
of letting them fall,

admiring their movement
in no particular direction.

I've been congested
a long while

nose in my belly
now breathes free

sniffing for adventure

leading me into unknown
right here

faraway future
calling on wires
I feel

but don't need to hear

this hunger
for more nothing

already filled

even as emptiness
deepens.

My sorrow
is your joy
moment of your giving

threshold to kindness
you touch with both hands

your grief
my nectar
sweetening life.

This story looked
like chaos,
wild imbalance of pain,
orbits of suffering
unhealthy

but now I sip
fresh water

feel descent and rise
as precious prostration

a dance of falling
caught by arms
that let us go

so our own
fly open.

I'm trying
to straddle
a tornado

live with my hips
open enough
to stand
and not be whirled away

spin wildly
in all the right places

and still
feel the eye of the storm

where soaring is.

Of course
I am knocked to the floor
almost every time

but can learn
from persistence
in his red hair

- whether I swear
or laugh,
I can try again.

Spanakopita

There were four triangles
resting under ice
in my freezer

left there at Christmas
when my sister,
who made them by hand,
went home.

I was prostrate
to listen

that day in the sun
before the grief welled up

and although meditation
sounds like sitting still
my body's wisdom
turned on the oven
waited for heat

let those four delicacies
warm my kitchen
then my belly.

So when the question arose
that prompted my sobs
knees on the ground

the sweet taste of salt
was already in my mouth

the tears added savour
to unravelled caring

all this love
pointless and deep

lonely
and connected.

Frozen poplars
lit at night

each twig frosted,
a sparkling coat
white against dark sky

layers of crystals,
a chemistry,
cold skyfall
roosting.

I was warm and waiting
in my car,
watching
what I thought I saw

until my gasp
woke me to their movement,
diamond branches dancing
wind rustling everywhere

and I still can hardly believe
I almost missed it.

Snails

If snails could speak

imagine the ponderous space

between utterings

slow soundings of kindness

freed from syllables

their headpieces

tasting wind

so near the earth

following no path,

leaving shiny trails

unnoticed

in their own view

carrying home

as a natural weight

bellies

propelled by ground

their words

in shapes

of silence.

He licks batteries
and the girl who stuck her tongue
in a wall outlet
knows intensity

knows longing to stand tall
in a field of lightening,
beckoning

knows damage
is inevitable.

Now these body scans
release new currents

diurnal scans
wring sweet juice
from everyday berries

the buzzing
of what is here
plugs me in
to a deeper source

pleasure and pain
notwithstanding.

Witness
to this healing

wounds open to air
have lost their fester,
are busy forming
healthy scars

a glow begins to flow
as the soldier on his back
enjoys his view of sky

life tingling.

I kiss his forehead
tenderly
and raise my glance
from this miracle

to bodies strewn
around us

roll my eyes to heaven,
wisdom laughter,

roll up our sleeves.

Help me shift
my posture

yes the alignment
of bones and flesh

liquid for the hunch
and clench

freedom from old habits
swimming in DNA.

Also my head,
incline of my days
- find the sweet spot
where standing tall
meets bowed in awe –

where voice and silence
both have room
for uttering.

Subtle adjustments,
let these small creakings
gap a space
for the rising sea on fire,

strong and porous vessel
for this throbbing heart.

Shame
like a wrecking ball
that did its work long ago
and hangs unmoving,
secure in its ponderous weight,
emanating cold.

I am so accustomed
to implied threat,
fear that it might swing

I tiptoe
in my creating,
build tents that leave no trace.

I have a list of reasons
why I deserve
to carry this chain
and heavy orb;
give me courage
to see where the links
connect to heart,
to let the fire of love
turn metal molten

let the old pendulum
be warmed
in the gentle gyrations
of my swinging hips.

These days
I'm a bit drunk
on living

tipsy with love
and nodding at lampposts

even deeper bows
in the face of friendships

the call of love
rings more pure
in this roomy cave
hollowed by time.

I'm still a little nervous
I might hiccup,
reveal inebriation
and make all you kind folk
uncomfortable
with my excesses

but I have pledged allegiance
to this wobble
and my valiant effort
to walk aligned.

Yum
and yuck

in one cycle
of breath

the illusion of truth

making liars of us all.

No place
to hang our hat;

even the most beautiful
hooks
are just molecules
briefly cohering.

Stark,
sad,
we prefer veils
to this view

but even blurred glimpses
melt frozen joy.

We're all so afraid
of ourselves

fear of our basement

the unlived stories
of our own destructive power

and so I follow the lead
of other brave souls with lamps

to see where my chained victims
are flayed in the dark.

I shine my candle
on my disloyalty,
her lush body
straining at the wall,
ready to flee
at the first offer of cake
or a surfboard
or a tantric glance.

Over here,
fear like a skinny child
pretends she can't breathe
so I will give pity,
plays at not enough
so I will give her
everything I have.

And here
my hatred
glows with righteous indignation,
heating up her chains
with flames of injustice,
seeking revenge
for all that is unfair.

Over here,
the blind one
wallows in her lack of vision,

unchained
but refusing to move.

I have built
such a door
against these harpies;
the path to the furnace
is blocked,
sentries are tired and cold,
none of us quite believing
in danger.

And so these faltering steps,
flickering light,
keys jingling,
looking for release
and warming fire.

Full moon
no wind
trees fat
in coats of snow

I walk in night
full of white light

rustling of my cares
the only breeze

not quite bowing
to these standing sisters
present in one place

passing through
their benedictions

circular driveway
back home
yet again.

Mostly I fear
the deep breathless beauty

of these fragile sandcastles
and how the water
keeps washing them away

and how love
moves my hands
as I kneel
by salty water

and tears fall
over my joyful fingers

my smiling heart
bowed
to the untouchable horizon

the grit and comfort
of this wet earth
in motion.

Oh, you little squirrel
scrambling to that branch
to announce danger

all that chittering
teaching me
to value peace

to laugh
at your frantic screams

telling me stories
of scolding and fear
all day long.

Help me
to move with grace
near your territory,
accept your shrill voice
as I stay tuned
to forest music.

Even me
with all these gifts

peace and safety
food and kindness
health and insights
friendships

deep love for nature's caress

even here
in all this freedom

my joy is itchy

the scratch of lack
prodding my search for solace

no relief

teaching me to sit
and feel

and welcome discomfort.

Let me sit
every morning

with pollen in the air

swirling grains
of possibility

knowing that some will land
and some travel.

I used to try
to craft my day
with lists;

let me open
my intentions

like freshly turned soil,

receiving gifts
that look like dust

watching for sprouts.

The shape of my peninsula
is not thrusting forward
into ocean,
stretching to a new edge
where cliff and water meet

but length is born
of erosion,
letting ocean cut my banks
shape my falling away
all day and night.

Harbourfront
and breakwater
slow the action
of these bays

but let me feel
how deeply
water presses inland,
receive the washing
as sand is scrubbed away

notice I am going nowhere
slowly

and still changing

how my stillness
will necessitate

new maps.

Any connection
is a miracle;

we trail these lengths
of unseen woven threads
that shape our every thought

sensations of pain
memories of pleasure
cringing and laughing
colours only we have seen
at certain heights
and angles of sun
through eyes
of changing widths

and using a word
includes all the choices
language
timing
fatigued or alert
laced with feeling

and whether the droplet
meets an open ear
or is lost in wind
or other noise

and the journey
for that sound
to move on buzzing paths
in other brains
with all their stories

to meet some kind meaning

heard as a greeting

… to earn
ten words together

or droplets enough
for a drink

... this is the awe
provoked by our being,
a joyful tip of the head
at any nod received.

Filaments

Raggedy cobweb
with big holes
where the pattern
was ripped

three dimensional
with no grand design,
a floating home
tossed in breeze

half in sunlight
and shadow too

anchored
and constantly changing

delicate
and strong

a net
for catching nourishment

guaranteed to break

and be rebuilt,

reconnect to the big world
where the spider lives.

I called myself lazy

because I was sitting

without the music,

too tired to find it.

Five different birdsongs

found their way

through an open window

at different moments

while the couch

held my slouch.

I have no words

to translate

mantra of birds.

Three different blooms
some wide
some buds

for too long
I have tried
fingers on petals
to force more opening

now I feel heat
on soil
and sucking roots

a heavy-lidded glance
to shapes around me

beauty unfolding
the way it will

petals cupping secret sky

or stamens waving gracefully

silk tenderness
floating to ground.

All this trembling
lets me know
love

the quaking body
that tries to hold still

and can't,

consumed by life
in full wobble

the crumbling
of useless barriers

protections that fall
in the shedding of certainty,

realness of light
exposing.

No doing,
just the barest whisper
to cells,
encouraging absorption

but of course
they know already

vibrations
of radiance

humming.

Hawking glimpses
of this hothouse

I sell tickets
and keep the glass clean
so you can peer
at all the beauty

and only enter
once a day
with shears and water

but lately the blooms
waft longing
even through glass

and succulent berries
call for my harvesting mouth

and there is enough light
to keep the door open

let me find a simple seat
in this moist air

no longer vendor
or caretaker

let awe
pour everywhere.

And you
silly woman
with headache
on the couch

trying to engage
with tomorrow's tomorrow
and all its cousins

invoking the best scenarios
even as you plot
to avoid the worst

a stream of fear and caring

let a squint
of humour
alter course
of the lines on your face

there really is
no tomorrow.

Fireflies
or comets
or elusive aurora

we yearn to capture light
to fill our jar
briefly

the quest
can be an endless suffering
of wanting more

or a rippling laughter
at our own small hands
raised under sky
that is.

How beautiful
to dance alone
and share sweet smiles in circle

listening to soundings
slower than time,

love like the long stories
mountains are rumbling.

Be more here

inside this skin

even as you feel
vast space
between your cells

be more here
in the cramp
of what keeps you small

feel how it is tight
and causes pain

and perfectly normal.

Feel the fear,
a snowball
inside

let its cold
melt into your veins

warmed and real

be more here.

There are times
that ask more of us,
demand our descent
to a pond
invisible and real

a place where visions
and sensations
share illusions of water
and we drink them

a place where we acknowledge
our crazy knowing
and trust in the fluid trans-rational.

This is the pond
where traffic is interrupted
by eagles
and only some
will bend their knees
or raise their arms

others will honk
and keep driving

but you are not alone
in your honouring;

keep attentive
to your awe.

A cook
with a well-stocked pantry

I have all these provisions,
so many flavours

help me to enter
my own domain

with curiosity
and just enough hunger

to keep tasting
all these combinations,

with just enough patience
to savour scent

enough trust
to let the stirring
move me.

Deep buzz
a tornado
swirls inside

the one I have feared
for so long

and is calling
with love that almost laughs

even as she scolds
for all the wasted moments.

The kunda wind
will burn
but not destroy

will shake and break
in service to love

will push unknown
into familiar

and safe
into strong breeze.

So many deaths
are possible

so many flavours
of storming
or greeting

the quaking calm
or still one

convulsions
or tender teardrops.

I was going to try
to pencil
my most beautiful intention

sketch a lovely end
pregnant with beginning

but see how this desire
wafts like steam rising
from tasting this real soup.

As if this briefcase
is too large

or my wheelchair

or bouffant hair piled high

or this armload
of other people's gear
and stinky socks

or even these shiny wings
taped to my shoulders;

every time
I approach the hole

feel the rough invitation
of boulders

there is something
to be dropped

so my real shape
fits the entry.

This body
my teabag

is steeped
right now

in hot water

those words
have triggered fear

and now laugh

as the dry leaves
warm in their birthright

sagging
into their vocation

surrendering to water

emanating flavour
without effort.

The house where I live
at night

has winding stairs
and ceilings too low to stand under

places where the steps
meet only a crawl space
even after ascending

floors that tilt
at odd angles

cozy little places
for hiding

rooms and hallways
full of people.

I know this place well
even as it changes every night

the contours of my soul
finding home.

Affection
as well as fear
lives here,

the comfort of familiarity
even in constant flux,
recognizing a story.

And for the first time
in the light
of a noisy dawn

I wonder why I need
all this complexity,

poke gently at the sense
of impending loss

my story bound up
in this large and rambling architecture,
recognizing me

when a hut
with a sliding roof
might also be
elegant sufficiency.

You're gonna be
an angel

someday soon

kindness in flight
merciful landings of feather

translucent in light

scattering seeds of joy.

Why not practice now
with the creaky sockets
where your wings will grow

the downturned droop
that wants uplifting?

Surely it will take
more than a few tries,
extending fingertips of love,
unfurling hope
like a hidden banner

and time is shrinkly

so why not now?

Every now and then
I'm shocked
by my own courage

a rabbit for years
scampering
timid
prolific and scattered

but see
how I pause
and twitch my nose

eyes red
from tears and cold

hiding in plain view,
not running.

That space
between the molecules
of gold

inside each cell

that tiny void
swimming without motion,
currents of vibration
all around

stillness repeated,
billions of small silences

all this buzzing emptiness
drawing me home.

Vocabulary of liberation

I have mostly
wiggled free
from the word
"should"

entangled
the net of my life
thinking in shoulds
— less space to receive
gifts of ocean.

today I choose
to stop dancing
with "could be"

a lonely minuet
with all its practiced steps
turning endlessly
pointlessly

today I feel
is
as much as I can
in feet and heart
and real sounds.

When will I wake up
to be fully alive?

Will it be a time in future
when I am vegan

or have cleaned all the closets;

when I communicate
in constant harmony;

when my body
feels no fear?

Or is there courage

to let clutter and decay

mingle with anxiety
and all the fierce not quite

like a splash of cool water

on a sleepy face?

Summertime sage
green on arid soil

your pungent beauty
touches my nose
when you are crushed
underfoot

this emanation
your invisible work
rooted in one place

no effort
in the way

sharing wisdom.

My ego screeches
warning

conflagration coming,
a wild hiss
of fire and water

making something new

hot steamy vague

no contours

pouring endlessly

burning the shapes
of what was.

Heart and mind
whisper kind touches

tin man melting
straw man long gone
lion on fire

roaring in protest

lost in flood.

Shaped by a song

childhood melody
of joy like rain,
laughter and clouds
falling in minor chords,
lamenting ode to the poignant.

I still sing
this rueful song

but let me also
greet stronger sunlight

feel the heat
of warm dry days

stop scanning for nimbus
not yet here

stretch in the feel of gold
under clear blue.

After 15 years
my fridge is loud

it speaks all day and night
mostly unheard;

in a quiet dawn
it teaches me

persistence

reminder of decay

the grace of plenty.

All in good time,

the time of goodness

finds me here,

faint buzzing of the lights

mirroring my thoughts,

bloodstream in motion,

restless calm.

That tree
with tender green leaves
soaring and spreading
out of reach

and hard smooth bark
with ridges
marked by time

I accept
the invitation to sit

my back supported,
leaning on life.

How long I stretched for fruits,
now swaying seeds

how long I tried to drink
sticky sap

this thrumming in my bum
from the dance of unseen roots

life coursing upwards
and flowing down

the tree at work
purifying the world
and me embraced
by joy,

a sacred slouch
that looks graceful

green light

going nowhere,

welcoming.

When the groaning stops,
becomes
a sigh of blessing

when the light flares
in flickers
even as it is waning

when our open sores
unlovely
teach us beauty

when our nausea
and grief
force our surrender

we bathe
in the kindness of the wounded.

Not quite crazy
I let myself be touched
by the freefalling void

the utter senselessness
of being alive
or dead

meaning
is just a convention,
syllables sounding
in a muscle
under a scalp

and somehow shared
occasionally
in almost-empty rooms.

Speaking of illusion
seems cruel

so we mask ourselves
in kind intention

and envy the freedom
of the naked.

Despite my yearning
for beauty in any form

what touches me
keeps peeling form away

roughly
gently

with each awkward
breath.

Learning With

My hand
outstretched in dark

I feel yours clasp
and the strength of it

girlfriend over decades…
the open shore
became this rocky cave.

How lovely
that my fear
of cold scrabbling,
of tiny spaces pressing in
and wet danger

has given way
to adventure

that my laughter
has room to bounce
as we crawl
and cling
and need prodding

the warm pool ahead
calling our very own names
so tenderly.

I am wedded
to the definite article

can you hear
the layers of laughter

how I need to excise
a certain grammar

even as I honour
a certain lifestyle.

And welcome too
uncertainty

an indefinite thread

an open-ended spice
flavouring this cake

a reverence for fragility

provoking humility.

If Buddha was a mom
she might not have picked
the bodhi tree

might have chosen instead
to keep wiping

noses and bottoms,
counters and floors,
walls, windows,
tear-streaked faces

gentle strokes of attention

resolved in her promise

to wipe with care

over and over

until enlightenment
propelled
more wiping.

My demons
are so friendly
they take up lots of space

hard to see,
the surgery is necessary
but my hand shakes

knowing I have slipped before,
have cut out shapes
that could have stayed

have let the laughing fellows
linger too long.

Let me renounce comforts
that keep me from living

give up cloying sweetness
for the simple kind

make more room
for what is real.

My wobbly wisdom
can't feel
whether I am more scared
of my beauty
or my ugly

whether my sinking
is deep release

whether my choice
to abandon hope
is what fuels light.

May I throw up my hands
even as I push against earth,
feel the pulsing
of my resistance
to gravity

live out this uncertainty
where grimace and grin
share space

collapse
on a planet
that keeps turning.

The earth's crust
is like my own

pretending to be solid
despite heaving waves
and undulating mountains

holding up little feet
that walk all over.

Molten at the core,
may I writhe
in fluid heat,
delight in the flow
of constant change

feel my plates
grind and slide

no blueprint
no problem

life alive.

This is what I make

…some craft meringues,
a deft touch and sweetness

or legislation
to save lives

clothing for warmth.

I make space
within my clutter

polish the sensors

a bio-receptor

tuned to life

ink
an echo of flow.

A large horse
with dependable hooves
gallops in surf

freed by motion,
hooves pounding
this tight band
under my ribs

fear and rebellion
churning up the shore
disrupting gentle waves

a necessary stomping

fear of exhilaration
meeting fear of surrender

snapping taut elastic

no destination

no rider, surfer
horse or waves

sand wet
and marked
by what passes.

No solace
in this warm body

or the one across the room

no solace
in this house
or the ways
of being paid

these comforts
like blankets
that slip.

So long
I've feared cold

but today the air
just meets my skin

planet breathing

my lungs too

spacious caress
neither warm nor cool

and everywhere.

Goddess of wild integrity
let me crawl
up your slippery slope

aware of the lush creations
I am crushing
because I cannot move
without touching what is here,

because my trail
leaves broken grass.

Help me to know
resilience

to slither humbly

to honour the green
tickling my belly

love beyond meaning

drawing me onwards

as real as I can be.

God will save me
except
there is no god

and in my truth
desolate terror

and one golden thread
fragile
persistent

binding belly
and heart

sliding past lips,
pores on my scalp

part of the weave
that ever was.

Sound of glass
smashing

some kinds of beauty
cannot be fixed

no happy ending

colour on the floor,
feet bleeding.

A story of hurt

and bitter waste

— let the cold breeze
enter my heart

chafing space
for truth.

Let me drop all hope
of redemption

and memory
of unbroken;

pause with my hesitation
to welcome ugly;

feel the liberation
of the deep is.

Cramp of indecision,
I get stuck in the choosing

me or them,
now or then,
which maybe
to pounce on.

And underneath,
am horrified
to feel a scrabbling,

crawling away from despair,

resisting the deep futility.

Let me fall
into this black hole
freely

feel the softness of void

how nothing matters

and there is no impact

in endless descent.

Extroverts
with hands raised
calling "Pick me!"

while introverts
subdue their hands
and call the same words
inside

and somewhere in noise
we stumble into silence

the quiet of the picked.

I choose blooming.

Oh I have been timid
like a maiden overripe,
a spinster
looking on the world
with longing

and also wise
beyond my years,
a crone
with dessicated dust
cupped in her hands,
a smile at futility

but only now
do I notice
how I turn my head
from deep perfume

pretend not to see
bright colour

ignore the fragile whorls
of delicate petals
growing around my core.

Even as I feel
tendrils of fear,
I see how they
have grown
to support my stem

and now there is strength
for this beauty

one heavy rich bloom
in an infinite garden

my nose
like one stamen
warmed by sun.

There's a rainbow
crawling up the window

some gift of glass
and refracted light;

I was craning to see the source
but don't need to.

Yellow and deep wounded indigo
bound with all the rest
for a few visible moments in time

in the vivid swath
a reminder

it is all here,
inseparable and distinct,
invisible and known.

I have been deaf
to my belly

today I let the listening
slide from my caring heart
with its murmurs of rejection
and the glow of its welcoming arms

let my ears fall low
to where they have been trying to hear
ancient wisdom,
a grounding articulate power.

Imagine my surprise
to find a creature
like a sheep

rumbling with contented need to feed,
inarticulate and sturdy;
a sound related to yum;
a mumble-thrum.

I knew the decades
of picking and choosing,
dry pasture

how simple and lovely
this ample grazing.

Let my eyes taste
movement of wind

let my nose hear
breeze

let my tongue feel
how it is skin
under breath

let my ears attune
to vibrations of colour

let my skin
absorb the scent
of sunlight on earth.

Someone once said
I was scolding
and they were right

now I sit
with a softer chiding
and hear
how I greet life
with admonitions

as if there was a curtain
I could reach behind
to pull out yet more treasures.

And while we do
hang cloth
to limit our view

let me just notice
how the panels
grow more sheer
with daylight

and how treasure
in this room now
is glinting
with light available.

A precious little puddle
I thought to protect

began to build a roof
as shrine

honouring wetness
behind a gate.

No miracle,
no Lourdes,
now I sit
dismantled

a soft depression
collecting rain

receiving
gifts of sky

licked
by wild things.

Me, I need to keep feeling nudged
by eager joy

like a dolphin
entranced by living
explores what is here

buoyed by its element,
bumping into friends,
hearing far-off sounds.

I know the fear
of floating,
my muscles a trained crew
rowing like mad
at the slightest wave

but the dolphin's
croaking grin
keeps inviting me
to swim.

Another cup of tea
a patient collecting
of dried bits
infusing them with heat,
light in the shape of water.

A patient brewing
even on a day
there is no time for it,
letting nostrils
do their unconscious work
in bringing awareness
to body
letting the flavour
of yesterday
permeate now
in a new blend.

I used to search
for the perfect cup,
delicate pursuit
of excellent elixir
to fill
a holy grail

and now this quest
is lost in fragrant steam

and knowing
the sweet taste
of these only leaves
in this temperature

and how yesterday
and tomorrow
will be different

feeling the not quite scalding
of water received.

Pain like a doorbell
inviting me
out
to play in the world

to taste what is here
awake

not wishing for more
or wanting less

but feeling the beautiful weight

cold scent of dawn

as I move to the summons
again.

There comes a day
that makes no sense

the whirring mind
cracks
and all the carrying
falls

meaning
turns to dust
in a dry mouth

and sorrow
seems vengeful.

But turn, my friend,
and rest your sad heart
on your fear

she will receive
your messy labour

help you birth
in weeping shame

a love
beyond understanding

a light that flickers
in the melting.

I don't have to find
my special brand of light

just open to the scooping
of eternal sun
even in darkness

nothing unique here
except the shape
of my own cramped hands
receiving.

This poem
is like a braided mat
handmade
by someone's grandma.

I pass it to you
rolled

and in your sense of place

you find a sacred patch;

you gently shake it out

and set it down
to pause
on its ragged colours

to feel imperfect lumps
and tender care

right now.

Afraid to exult
in this delicious life

I delay
my own joy

pretending that's wisdom.

These rivulets of wonder
are tickling my soul
provoking the undignified throb
of giggling

consummate yes!!

with exclamation marks.

Let me gallop
even with a flabby ass

let me huff and tingle
most ungracefully

let me transform
from moth
to wick
on fire.

If I try
to get to God
through you

I'll get lost
in strange terrain

pushing at boulders
I don't recognize

my feet uncertain.

I have spent time
trying to clear your path

and while perhaps
I got stronger
with useless pushing,

now I fondle my own stones
with familiar tenderness

and feel how light finds me
on this winding, rocky trail.

I'm amazed
by the kindness
in this pruning

how necessary snips
do cut me
and I can hear growth
falling to ground
even with quiet sound.

Not just benign,
I feel the caring,
touch of unseen fingers
stretching past my thorns
to trim all this excess.

Crooked, wilted,
fragrant, fresh

no perfection,

gratitude for shears.

Sitting
I stumbled
on muscles
in my middle

trying so hard to
trying hard
trying to

and with a whisper
of reminding

those muscles
stayed about the same

but I could feel skin
on old upholstery

and knew the couch
was held by a room
in a big world
with everything in it.

Boats with holes
will sink

and tho' we are all ocean
trying to swallow our boats

this precious life
begs us to float

to pour warm oil
on leaky seams

scrape off habits
like barnacles

mount our sails
to catch inconstant wind.

And yes
I feel ocean in you
and you and you

but I will get lost
if I dribble through my cracks

instead let me shout joyfully
as you move nearby

and feel what carries us all.

That time
fruit flies
were plentiful

clouds of curious beings
probing our decay
our sweetness

we spent precious life force
enticing them
to an early demise

despite their meandering,
circuitous path,
refusal to play
our logical game.

May my
inevitable fermentation
be freed
from its toxic harming,

waft through our home,
inducement to joy.

Once upon
a glassblower
worked alone
– oh, friends brought fuel
for the fire
and helped her collect
the different sands

but she lit the flames
each morning
and felt the heat
and blew her breath
on molten mixtures

joy in fragile baubles
catching light.

She hung them all around
inside her walls
and folks would venture
to her door
and leave smiling.

There was a knight
in shining armour
with a strong visor
and galloping stallion
and piercing lance

she loved to watch his beauty riding free,
protecting the village
from dragons.

Sometimes
inevitable crashing
marked the sound of her welcome,
horse and armour
too large to fit,
visor in the way
of seeing her work,
lance knocking glass
without intention.

She learned to laugh
and sweep;
he learned to leave protections
at the door;
she also learned
to hang her craft
on outside trees
and sit in sunlight
for their trysts.

Sisters
by our choice
in men

I sit a world away
like an old woman
wrapped in a blanket

and my face drips
for our shared sorrow
you carry.

We knew more
of each other
than was polite

and so our sharing
had averted eyes

respect and also fear

but oh! my heart is sad
and face crumpling

with your broken hero
gone.

We talk of path

as if we need to travel

as if we are lost and need movement

today I feel the path

in my body

the way I can block the light

trying to journey

the precious glow of love

patiently stepping around my boulders

scrambling through scree.

I am path

for life

finding its way

here.

Lea-Ann
might have dressed that bird
just so

I would not have courage
to put that golden green
with white and black and blue

but what beautiful drama
for the eye

evolution
playing with possibility

form and function
sorting themselves out

endlessly.

A dripping tap
sounds like a clock
on speed
insistent

my toe pokes through
a surprising hole
in a new sock

the houseplants
need turning,
leaning with devotion
towards a sun that teases,
needing my help
to regain their dignity

like orgasm,
I so often rush
to a conclusion

today I can sit
with perplexing pleasure.

Blurry diamonds
those drops
on the dead tree
were here all along

they glisten
as I listen
to the angle of sun
mixing with surf song
and birds
in constant practice

tuning up
for the orchestral now

grey sky
notwithstanding

sunlight
in vivid refractions

fairie lights
in daytime

no magic
except the real kind

always hiding
here.

Captain
of my ship

I sniff air
for danger

and even reports
from my team
of all this smooth sailing

and even
calm glassy sea
and joyful birdcalls

not quite enough
for me to soften.

May my stance
on these sunlit waves
allow a little jig,
a chat with cook,
a fingering of silks in the hold.

Sea change flows always
and captains can be ready
without standing guard.

My soul
a balloon
trying to sip helium

to expand and float

while ego howls
its beacon of dread

and keeps applying
fresh strips of paper and glue.

I'm so glad
this paper-maché
stays damp,
ego working daily
to keep me small

soul stretching gently
the space for emptiness

both of them creating
this changing shape.

All these longings
especially those
I don't even know
until I burst in tears
or feel electricity,
total shock

… and the polished ones,
burnished by long habit

… let me honour
beautiful aches

even as I open
my fragile fingers

watch them fall,
dissolved by ocean

glint on surface
like diamonds not there.

That muddy statue
had been loved
for years

received the gifts
of so many

offered solace
in its silence,
even unlovely

until worn down by time
a crack in its façade
and a curious monk
with a light

revealed its solid gold.

So too
may I wield
my flashlight
on all this lumpy life

sure already
of what lies underneath

receiving mud
and cracking
with the tenderness
of gold on offer.

www.ingramcontent.com/pod-product-compliance
Lightning Source LLC
Chambersburg PA
CBHW071816020426
42331CB00007B/1502